2001

W9-CCF-700

What to Do

When You Don't
Know What to Say

OUR FATHER'S LIBRARY
36 W 2ND
PERU, IN 46970

Books by
Mary Ann Froehlich
AND
PeggySue Wells

Holding Down the Fort

What to Do When You Don't Know What to Say

What to Do

When You Don't
Know What to Say

MARY ANN FROEHLICH

& PEGGYSUE WELLS

❖ BETHANY HOUSE
Minneapolis, Minnesota

What to Do When You Don't Know What to Say
Copyright © 2000
Mary Ann Froehlich and PeggySue Wells

Cover design by Eric Walljasper
Cover illustration by Todd Williams

Scripture quotations identified NIV are from the HOLY BIBLE, NEW INTERNATIONAL VERSION®. Copyright © 1973, 1978, 1984 by International Bible Society. Used by permission of Zondervan Publishing House. All rights reserved. The "NIV" and "New International Version" trademarks are registered in the United States Patent and Trademark Office by International Bible Society. Use of either trademark requires the permission of International Bible Society.

Scripture quotations marked NEB are from *The New English Bible*. Copyright © 1961, 1970 by the delegates of the Oxford University Press and the syndics of the Cambridge University Press.

Scripture quotations marked NJB are from *The New Jerusalem Bible*. Copyright © 1998, 1999 by Random House, a division of Doubleday.

All rights reserved. No part of this publication may be reproduced, stored in a retrieval system, or transmitted in any form or by any means—electronic, mechanical, photocopying, recording, or otherwise—without the prior written permission of the publisher and copyright owners.

Published by Bethany House Publishers
A Ministry of Bethany Fellowship International
11400 Hampshire Avenue South, Bloomington, Minnesota 55438
www.bethanyhouse.com

Printed in the United States of America by
Bethany Press International, Bloomington, Minnesota 55438

Library of Congress Cataloging-in-Publication Data

What to do when you don't know what to say : helping in times of crisis /
[compiled] by Mary Ann Froehlich & PeggySue Wells.
      p. cm.
   ISBN 0–7642–2371–2
   1. Helping behavior–Religious aspects–Christianity.   I. Froehlich, Mary
Ann, 1955–   II. Wells, PeggySue.
   BV4647.H4 W48 2000
   253—dc21
                                                              00–009845

MARY ANN FROEHLICH is a registered music therapist and author of several books. She has a doctorate in music and a master's degree in pastoral care and lives in California with her husband and three children.

PEGGYSUE WELLS is a homemaker, teacher, graphic artist, editor, and writer. She and her husband make their home in Indiana with their seven children.

Dedicated to our precious families
and our dear friends
who have faithfully been
the hands of Christ
in our lives.

Acknowledgments

We offer heartfelt thanks to our many contributors who graciously shared how others came alongside them during the crises of their lives. We are grateful to Ann Parrish, Steve Laube, and our friends at Bethany House for catching the vision and bringing this project to completion.

Contents

Introduction

The pride of a small town in Europe was their statue of Jesus in the village square. During World War II the town was bombed. The townspeople collected the pieces of the destroyed statue and painstakingly did their best to re-create it. When they finished gluing the statue back together, the only pieces missing were the hands of Jesus. They placed a plaque at the base of the statue with the message:

Now we are the only hands that Jesus has.

How can we be Jesus' hands to our friends and neighbors who are experiencing crisis in their lives? Our desire to help is sincere but we sometimes don't know how. "How can I help?" is a fruitless question. In the pit of emotional or physical pain, people do not have the energy to tell us what would help them. True help comes from feeling someone's pain, seeing a need, and acting on that insight.

Helping is the ministry of enCOURAGEment, to give someone courage in their darkest hour. The goal of helping is to come alongside and bear our friends' heartaches with them. Helping, as defined by Webster, is to support, make more bearable, relieve, benefit, and change for the better.

People are often most helped when one person takes the time to "give them a hug from God"—one single, often invisible act that provides an anchor in the stormy waters of despair. A loving deed performed by someone who cares for us is "Jesus with skin on."

Through the years PeggySue and I have been listening, always anxious to hear what truly helps people when they hurt. We listened for unique ideas beyond making a phone call or sending a card. The inspiration for many of my books came from a single statement made by a seminary professor of mine twenty years ago. He said, "I think that we should close the textbooks and theological treatises and simply ask people, 'How did you survive that? How did God carry you through that ordeal?'"

Intended to inspire you on your journey of helping, this collection of real-life experiences is an idea book. These ideas were compiled from numerous anonymous contributors who shared what helped them most during a difficult time in their lives. In an effort to make it easier for readers to access the ideas relating to a specific situation, we have grouped them under separate categories. We encourage you to read all the entries in a particular chapter because many of these ideas can be applied in a variety of circumstances. This is not a book about professional help. Friends are not a substitute for therapy, nor is therapy a substitute for friendship.

Difficult times are a fact of life. You've probably already experienced your share. And the future likely holds additional challenges for you and those you love. Christ tells us, "In this world you will have trouble. But take heart! I have overcome the world" (John 16:33b NIV). May we never forget our privileged calling of daily mirroring Jesus Christ and being His helping hands to a hurting world.

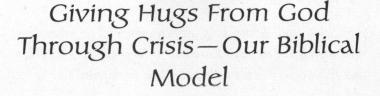

CHAPTER ONE

Giving Hugs From God Through Crisis — Our Biblical Model

God knows how to lead us to the point of crisis, and He knows how to lead us through it. . . . There is no way out but God.

—L. B. COWMAN

Crisis has many faces in our lives including losing a loved one, facing a serious illness, an addiction problem, a job change, relocation, or divorce. Some crises are devastating, changing our lives forever. Others are stressful but eventually bring beneficial outcomes. Crisis often causes us to start over. All crises can feel overwhelming.

By definition, a crisis is a turning point. People in crisis can feel helpless and desperate. They live on the edge of hopelessness, often feeling powerless to change their situation. The stress is paralyzing. In the Chinese language, the characters that represent crisis signify danger or opportunity. A crisis can destroy someone or it can make that person stronger. The turning point comes in how we face the crisis—and how we face the crisis often depends on what kind of support we receive.

> *Oh, how shall I find help within myself? The power to aid myself is put out of my reach. Devotion is due from his friends to one who despairs and loses faith in the Almighty.*
>
> JOB 6:12–13 NEB

God promises His children that the crises in our lives will not destroy us. He will be there to comfort and carry us through difficult times. The Holy Spirit is also referred to as the Paraclete (from the Greek word *parakletos*), meaning the comforter who comes alongside to aid or support, the advocate. Coming alongside to comfort others is our biblical model for ministry.

> *We are hard pressed on every side, but not crushed; perplexed, but not in despair; persecuted, but not abandoned; struck down, but not destroyed. We always carry around in our body the death of Jesus, so that the life of Jesus may also be revealed in our body.*
>
> 2 CORINTHIANS 4:8–10 NIV

Gifts of the Heart

> *A gift opens the door to the giver and gains access to the great.*
>
> PROVERBS 18:16 NEB

The theme that runs through these real-life experiences is a gift that can take many forms. Opening the door to healing, to relationship, to faith, a gift is an offering given with no compensation. We desire nothing in return. These are not gifts that can be purchased in a store as celebrated in our culture. Not dependent on our resources, these are gifts of time, compassion, and sensitivity. People who have the least amount of time and money often give the most to others. The gifts described in these pages come from the heart and bring the message: "I know and recognize your pain. You are not alone. I am here."

The Chain of Compassion

We are the links in God's chain of compassion. He comforts us in our sufferings so that we will be able to comfort others.

> *Blessed be the God and Father of our Lord Jesus Christ, a gentle Father and the God of all consolation, who comforts us in all our sorrows, so that we can offer others, in their sorrows, the consolation that we have received from God ourselves. Indeed, as the sufferings of Christ overflow to us, so through Christ, does*

*our consolation overflow. When we are made to suffer,
it is for your consolation and salvation.*

2 CORINTHIANS 1:3–6 NJB

We are most aware of the suffering of another when we have personally experienced the same pain. Experience is the spectacles God gives to help us see clearly. The experience of suffering refines us into gold. No one knows the pain of losing a child like other parents who have suffered the same loss. Only a widow truly understands the despair of other newly widowed women, and the man best able to help a friend who just lost his job is one who has also been unemployed. The critical piece in helping others is the ability to see and feel their pain, to truly understand what the person in crisis is enduring. We have a God who personally consoles and revives us in our despair and He chooses to use individual people as links in His chain of comfort:

For when we came into Macedonia, this body of ours had no rest, but we were harassed at every turn—conflicts on the outside, fears within. But God, who comforts the downcast, comforted us by the coming of Titus, and not only by his coming but also by the comfort you had given him.

2 CORINTHIANS 7:5–7A NIV

You are an agent of comfort, an indispensable link in God's chain of compassion. As you read the following contributions, remember your own painful experiences of crisis, how

God comforted you, and how others helped or did not help you. Our Savior calls us to carry one another's burdens.

Chances to be Angels

It isn't the thing you do, dear,
It's the thing you leave undone
That gives you the bitter heartache
At the setting of the sun;
The tender word unspoken,
The letter you did not write,
The flower you might have sent, dear,
Are your haunting ghosts at night.
The stone you might have lifted
Out of your brother's way,
The bit of heartfelt counsel
You were hurried too much to say;
The loving touch of the hand, dear,
The gentle and winsome tone,
That you had no time or thought for,
With troubles enough of your own.
These little acts of kindness
So easily out of mind,
These chances to be angels,
Which even mortals find—
They come in nights of silence,
To take away the grief;
When hope is faint and feeble,

And a drought has stopped belief.
For life is all too short, dear,
And sorrow is all too great,
To allow our slow compassion
That tarries until too late.
And it's not the thing you do, dear,
It's the thing you leave undone,
That gives you the bitter heartache
At the setting of the sun.

—ADELAIDE PROCTOR

CHAPTER TWO

In Times of Illness

Indeed he was ill, and almost died. But God had mercy on him, and not on him only but also on me, to spare me sorrow upon sorrow.

—PHILIPPIANS 2:27 NIV

Chronically ill for months, I missed being able to fill our home with the smell of Christmas cookies fresh from the oven. We bought cookies at the bakery, and friends would bring them, but it just wasn't the same as our yearly tradition of home-baking. When my friend sent her teenagers over for an afternoon to bake cookies with my children, the aroma and festivities of baking lifted my spirits.

My husband was away on a business trip when my

children and I came down with the flu. My friend left a "cold care package" on our porch containing Kleenex tissues, throat lozenges, cold medication, herbs, and tea. She was a lifesaver when I couldn't get to the store.

After I was diagnosed with a serious illness, my friend drove me to every doctor's appointment and sat with me while I waited. The illness was overwhelming, but I didn't face it alone. My friend was my guardian angel with skin on.

Surgery saved my husband's life. As I sat by his bedside during his recovery, I was delightfully surprised when a deliveryman arrived. My friend had arranged to have dinner brought in from our favorite restaurant. She knew this was an important occasion for us to celebrate and that we would be too exhausted to do anything for ourselves.

Though I am forty-four years old, my mother still brings homemade chicken noodle soup and biscuits whenever one of us is sick. I don't know if it is the soup or purely her love, but this special meal helps cure us every time.

After going through a battery of tests and a biopsy for cancer, I returned home to find a bouquet of flowers on my porch. The attached note assured me that my friend had been thinking about me through the draining process.

I ran in a marathon and collapsed on the finish line. Friends at the race took our children home with them so my wife could ride with me in the ambulance. My close friend and his wife followed the ambulance and stayed with my wife and me at the hospital until I was out of danger. God sent many angels to help us that day.

A back injury left me in severe pain, not to mention feeling completely useless to my family and quite depressed. My friends went into action. One friend cleaned my house each week. Another friend took my weekly list to the market. One drove my children to and from school, and another organized meals for us. These special friends divided the load and each shouldered a part. Like the friends who brought the crippled man to Jesus, they helped carry me through a difficult time.

Hospitalized during my daughter's seventh birthday, I longed to make her birthday special, but I was powerless to even get out of bed. My friend understood my mother's heart. She phoned to ask what my daughter wanted for her birthday. Later that day, she came to my room to deliver my daughter's wrapped gift, a store-bought birthday cake, and paper goods. Before she left, she hung streamers and balloons. When my husband and children arrived, my sterile hospital room had been transformed into a party. The birthday I feared would be a bad memory for my daughter remains one of our family's favorite days, thanks to my thoughtful friend.

I have a terminal illness. As a mom, I am most concerned about leaving my children. Since my husband needs me, too, we planned a trip to Mexico, our last getaway together. Because of the complications of my illness, our good friends accompanied us to help. They were open to talking about my impending death and arrangements for the future. Now I have the comfort of knowing my friends will be there for my family when I am gone.

The chicken pox rotated among my four children. Being housebound for two months made us feel like we were suffocating. My friend brought over a "sick basket" loaded with games, movie videos, toys her children had outgrown, art supplies, and other activities. It was better than Christmas.

Due to a stroke, my father became difficult, even abusive, to our family and especially to my mother. I tried to help my mother care for him, but I couldn't bear to watch his deterioration. The pain he was inflicting on his loved ones was something he never would have intentionally done. When I would get to the end of my rope, I would run to my friend. She hugged me and spoke sweet words of comfort. Those words were pillows for my hurt. Because of her, I could persevere.

A friend came to sit with me in the hospital after my surgery for cancer. It was the darkest day of my life. She was a new Christian, and God spoke to me through her when she said, "I think that you're going to have to let some of your friends carry your pain for you." She comforted me with that single sentence of hope. Later when other friends of ours lost their child, my husband and I found it awkward to contact them. We wanted to avoid their pain. But from my friend's example we knew that we simply needed to be there. We took a deep breath and called them.

When I was hospitalized for many weeks, one friend brought me foods I enjoy and could stomach. Another friend came to read aloud to me. On the days she couldn't come in person, she equipped me with a battery-operated tape player and audiobooks. Listening to the cheery stories on cassette encouraged me and helped pass the time.

When my husband was hospitalized due to heart problems, my Bible study group organized meals and child care for our family so I could be at the hospital. Some of the women visited my husband and prayed with him. They anticipated our needs and met them before we were even aware of what they were. God used these angels to draw my husband into a personal relationship with Him.

Now that we live in a small town, I sometimes still miss the big city. After my hysterectomy, I was feeling blue. My girlfriend, who lives in another state,

called a local caterer to arrange an elegant dinner to
be delivered to us in our home. I was overcome
with joy.

Born with serious heart defects, our baby required
emergency surgery. I was consumed with caring for
my newborn in his critical condition. Knowing I
needed a break but would never leave my son alone
in the hospital, our friends came to sit with my son
so my husband and I could go out for a quiet dinner. I will always remember their act of kindness.

My husband broke his back in an automobile accident and was confined to bed. Every Saturday, his
friend from work came over to visit and catch him
up on the week's events. His wife brought a picnic
basket filled with lunch goodies, and their children
played with our children. Looking forward to Saturday helped us get through the rest of the week. Our
friends were busy people, but they made us a priority during a bleak time in our lives.

Isolation at home adds depression to my chronic illness. Knowing that I am too weak to drive, my
friend takes me on short outings to get something

to eat or buy a new nightgown. My pastor sends his taped messages to me weekly so that I can still feel plugged into our church family. It is a great comfort to know I am not "out of sight, out of mind" and forgotten.

My illness requires frequent emergency hospitalizations. My friend makes herself available around the clock to rush me to the hospital whenever I need to be admitted. She stays with me when I see the doctor, asks the doctor questions I am too panicked to think of, and writes the doctor's instructions down so I can refer to them later. She has even spent the night with me in the hospital when the nursing staff has been overworked. Her gentle presence is my stability.

Knowing that the surgeon might find a cancerous tumor, I was frightened about my upcoming surgery. I also dreaded not being able to eat for days afterward. My husband and friends gave me a party on the eve of surgery. Their funny cards, gifts, and delicious food cheered me and kept my mind from becoming consumed with fear.

My grandfather was an invalid, yet every week he wrote at least one letter to someone who was suffering. Each lengthy, heartfelt letter was filled with encouragement, the wisdom of personal experience, and Scripture verses. I know about his ministry not only because I often bought his stationery and mailed the letters but also because I was sometimes the recipient of a love letter when I was having a tough time. He not only reached out to countless people in his later years but writing those letters gave his own life purpose and direction. Encouraging others proved to be the best medicine for him.

Raising a child with special needs is a difficult round-the-clock task. For years a friend visited once a week to play games, sing, create art projects, and simply love my child. I counted on that one afternoon every week to have a break. I could return to my labor of love refreshed, and my child always had a smile on her face after spending time with my friend.

My daughter was active in dance and various sports. When a skiing accident left her a paraplegic, we mourned the loss of her normal life almost as much as a death. Watching her suffer was the most painful part of our grief. She was filled with anger and didn't want to live. When many of our daughter's friends eventually stopped visiting because they couldn't stand to see her in that state, one friend consistently came to visit no matter how my daughter lashed out at her or how depressed we were. It wasn't enjoyable to spend time with us in our isolation, but our friend's faithfulness never wavered. Sometimes she brought my daughter's favorite foods, a desired book, video, CD, or other items that acknowledged my daughter was still the same person inside.

When my husband's ninety-two-year-old grandmother became too ill to live alone, we did not want to place her in a nursing facility. We brought her to our home to care for her, a task that was overwhelming at times. She was upset with the world, and she directed her anger toward me. One friend faithfully took the time to listen to my tale of woes. Another friend came weekly to trim and style Grandma's hair. Our pastor visited with her regularly and always gave me words of encouragement when he left. These acts of kindness felt like a hug from God.

I quickly grew weary of hospital food while I stayed with my sick child in the pediatric ward. My friend brought me home-cooked meals when she came to visit. I appreciated her extra effort in helping me stay strong for my child.

I was a drug addict living on the streets. Through a church connection, a family invited me to live in their home after I had tried to take my own life. I was very unlovable, but they fed me, provided shelter, helped care for my new baby, and set boundaries for me. They showed me what a loving family looks like and helped me start a new life.

The hours dragged when I was in the hospital. Knowing how ugly I felt and how lonely I was, my friend came to give me a manicure. Her companionship and pampering was the best medicine I had.

My illness affects our entire family. When my husband is overloaded at work, one friend drives me to my doctor appointments. Another friend makes sure that my children are included in fun activities such as going to the park, the library, concerts, music lessons, sports activities, and 4-H meetings. Because my friends care, my children don't have to feel isolated by my illness.

Due to complications, I spent a good portion of my pregnancy on bed rest. Each week a friend came to clean my home while our preschoolers played. She would leave me a supply of uplifting videos and a favorite book until she returned the following week.

Our child was seriously ill when my husband lost his job. Our medical insurance would quickly expire. We had no prospects for a new job, and there was little hope that a future insurance carrier would cover our child's existing medical condition. For as long as we needed it, friends arranged to pay the monthly charge to keep our family's current policy active. When our world was falling apart, I was able to count on my son's receiving the health care he needed.

When helping someone, it is more important to bring hope than to be an expert.

—Pat Palau

(breast cancer survivor)

CHAPTER THREE

In Times of Loss and Grief

Save me, O God: for the waters have risen up to my neck.
I sink in muddy depths and have no foothold; I am swept
into deep water, and the flood carries me away. I am
wearied with crying out, my throat is sore, my eyes grow
dim as I wait for God to help me.

—PSALM 69:1–3 NEB

My dad died on a Wednesday. Every Wednesday
throughout the first year of my grief, I found garden flowers and encouraging notes on my porch.
My friend's weekly gift spoke to my heart: *"I re-*
member your pain. Hope in the spring to come during
the winter of your soul."

After my husband's death, my friend came to help

35

me clean out his clothes from our closet. I couldn't have faced that task alone, as the memories of each item I held brought me to tears. My friend packed up his clothes for me and took them away. I assumed she would deliver them to a local charity organization. One month later, she presented me with a quilt she had made from all his clothes. That gift is my treasure.

Though I lost my mother in the autumn, the wound was still fresh the following spring. When everyone else was sending Mother's Day greetings, my friend sent me a card, letting me know that she shared my sorrow and loss. She understood how difficult that day would be for me.

When my young daughter was dying of cancer, my friend would often take my other children out for ice cream or to the movies. She knew that I couldn't leave my daughter but understood the need for her siblings to experience normal childhood fun.

My father did not survive surgery and he died at midnight. We held his body and cried until we had to leave the hospital. My mother's best friend—my adopted aunt—stayed with us throughout the entire ordeal. Then she took us to her home and prepared a beautiful tea party, served on her best china, at 3:00 A.M. I have never attended a more fitting tea party. It was an oasis for our family between the trauma and the deep grief to follow.

Life was overwhelming after my wife died. I felt lost. I couldn't even go to the market because that was a task that she had always done. I didn't know what detergent to buy. I dreaded seeing foods that I knew were her favorites. A close friend offered to come with me on my first trip to the grocery store. He was my shelter from the raging storm.

After my twelve-year-old son died, an elderly friend invited me over for lunch. She told me something that she had never shared with anyone before. Fifty years ago she had lost her four-year-old son in an accident, and she still grieved for him. She wanted me to know that it was perfectly normal that I would never "get over it." Only another parent who had lost a child could truly understand the intensity of my pain.

When I was a teenager, my father and brother were killed in an accident just weeks before Christmas. In her grief, my mother could not face celebrating Christmas. Yet I needed some normalcy, some tenuous sense of family tradition in my suddenly upside-down world. My friends from the high school band purchased a tree, brought it to our home, and decorated it. I am forty-five years old now, and I have never forgotten how that one thoughtful act eased my hurt during that tragic holiday season.

Our long-awaited baby died in utero. Men typically don't seek out someone to talk to, and I was feeling angry, sad, and very much alone. As soon as my friend heard the news, he came directly to my office and took me out to lunch. He understood that I needed to talk to someone. My friend listened, and he prayed with me. He showed me there was someone, another man, who cared how I was feeling.

The first Valentine's Day after my husband's death intensified how deeply I missed the love of my life. In despair, I went into my bedroom and cried out to the Lord. At that moment, there was a knock on the door. There stood my friend with a beautiful bouquet of flowers. I fell into her arms crying, so grateful that God had not forgotten me.

My daughter had a terminal illness, and we celebrated her last birthday in the hospital. Friends sent a birthday box to our room complete with streamers, balloons, paper products, a cake, and everything else we needed for a party. We needed to savor her last birthday.

My friend did not send flowers to my mother's memorial service. Instead, she sent them to me two months later on my mother's birthday. By then most people had forgotten about my grief, but my friend knew my pain would still be intense the weeks and months following my mother's death.

My father died a few weeks before Christmas, a very hard time to lose a loved one. While we spent our last days with him in another part of the state, a good friend cared for our home. She left a poinsettia plant, a small glimpse of Christmas, on the kitchen counter to greet us when we returned home. One year later, on the anniversary of my dad's death, my friend left another poinsettia plant on our porch. She remembered us in our grief during both of those holiday seasons.

A close friend made a quilt and brought it to my husband's funeral for everyone to sign with their favorite memory of him. When the grief becomes unbearable, I can literally wrap myself in our memories.

When my daughter died, my friend gave me a journal. She knew it would be helpful for me to write letters to my little girl. I wrote often in the beginning, and now I write annually on my daughter's birthday. More important, my friend said that I could read the letters to her at any time. My spouse and family members couldn't bear to hear my pain. I needed someone outside my family to listen to these words from the depths of my heart.

When my sister lay dying of cancer, I moved in to care for her and her three children. It was a terribly hot summer, and money was tight. One friend installed a bedroom air-conditioning unit and brought over fans for the other rooms. Another friend quietly paid the power bill each month. As I labored to put my sister's affairs in order, friends would drop by with much-needed postage stamps. My sister was daily cheered by greeting cards that came in the mail. As I cared for my sister, friends delivered meals. I am thankful for these dear people who understood when my sister was too ill to visit but found other ways to minister to her needs. They respected her fragile dignity.

After my son's death, I couldn't bear to enter his room. I couldn't even think of cleaning it out. Finally I faced the task. My friend was there every step of the way, giving clothes and toys to needy children, donating books to the library, taking games to the hospital where my son had been a patient, and making sure every item would bring happiness to another child. That is how I wanted it, but I didn't have the strength to make it happen. She packed my son's favorite stuffed animals and the blanket that he slept with in a little suitcase for me to keep. Those possessions have given me sweet comfort the days my arms ache to hold my son again.

My brother lived with us so we could care for him while he was dying from AIDS. When we were emotionally and physically exhausted, our friends cared for us so we could care for him. One friend took me out for an afternoon ice cream break. Another friend came to read to my brother. One came to play music, and another made all our travel arrangements when my brother needed to see a doctor in another state. They all came alongside us to love him.

Watching my husband die a slow, painful death to cancer broke my heart. Knowing that my husband couldn't do it, my friend sent flowers on Valentine's Day. She made sure I was not forgotten on that last holiday for lovers.

It was the Christmas season when my father died after emergency heart surgery. My closest childhood friend purchased an angel ornament for me, but when she went to wrap it, she found that it was cracked across the heart. Someone else might have thrown the ornament away, but she glued it back together and sent the "brokenhearted" angel in memory of my dad's broken heart. Every time I see that ornament, I remember how my friend shared my pain during that dark time.

Every day I have to drive the same highway on which my children were killed in an auto accident. Passing the scene of the crash will always be painful, but it helps that friends still leave flowers and notes there in their memory. No one can take my pain away, but dear friends do help it hurt less. I'm glad others remember my children.

I was close to my dad, so his sudden death was devastating. All my friends were very supportive, but there was no substitute for those few who had also recently lost their dads. They cried with me, and they wrote letters to me describing their experiences that mirrored mine. I was comforted because my friends literally felt my pain.

When my two teenagers were killed in an auto accident, I was too numb to search the Scriptures for comfort. My friend bought me a beautiful devotional Bible and highlighted passages to minister to my pain. In my paralysis, I could simply open my Bible and see my friend's markings. Those words were my hope.

Cherry pie was my husband's favorite dessert. After he died, my friend brought me a cherry pie every year on his birthday. She turned a sad day into a celebration of memories shared over cherry pie and coffee. I have learned to be grateful for the time I had with my husband instead of bitter about losing him.

After our daughter died, a teenage hospital volunteer wrote us a letter expressing how our daughter had touched her life. We were grateful to know our young daughter had made a positive impact on someone else during her short lifetime. I cherish that letter.

When our baby was born dead, no one knew what to say. We were weary of hearing, "At least . . ." One friend simply gave us a rosebush to plant in our baby's honor, saying, "Your rosebud has bloomed on the other side of the fence—in eternity." My baby's life had value, no matter how short her time with us.

Involved in illegal activities, my father had not lived an exemplary life. When he was murdered, we did not receive an outpouring of sympathy. Some people felt that my father had gotten what he deserved. Ignorant of our suffering, no one in our church sent a card or flowers. The few cards we received came from longtime friends. Those cards were lighthouses in an ocean of grief. These sensitive friends understood that our tears did not stop when the funeral was over.

Thrilled to be pregnant with our third child, I woke up in the middle of the night and knew that something was terribly wrong. My husband rushed me to the hospital, where I miscarried our baby. I was left to recover in a hospital room, listening to the joyful exclamations of mothers who had just birthed their living babies. It was raining when my husband was finally allowed to drive me home. Physically I was wet, cold, and shivering. Emotionally I was numb with grief. Waiting for me at home, a friend had prepared my bedroom, turned down the bed, and turned on the electric blanket. She didn't say anything. Tucked in my own warm bed, I could safely grieve. Years have passed, but when I face a difficult situation, I remember sliding into the warmth of a bed prepared by my caring friend, and I am comforted.

News came that my father was dying. I did not have the funds to fly home. My Bible study group collected enough money for my plane ticket and even gave me a ride to the airport. I was living in a fog of sorrow, but these dear friends took care of every detail.

After my child died, well-intentioned friends tried to say just the right thing. But there are no right words. One friend simply cried with me regularly. She knew that there was nothing to say. I heard once that what hurting people need most is a "shared lump in the throat"—nothing more, but nothing less.

A precious co-worker was killed in an auto accident a month before a major presentation. My boss gave each team member a small stone to keep in our pockets during presentation week. When our sorrow overwhelmed us, the stones were intended to remind us that God would bring us through this tragedy just as He brought the Israelites through the Jordan River. The Israelites stacked stones to remember God's faithfulness through difficult times.

Later my boss mailed her stone to a friend whose child had been killed in an auto accident. That friend kept the stone in her purse for a year as a tangible reminder that God would see her through her grief. When she was ready, she passed the stone to someone else who was struggling. There was nothing magical in the stone; it merely reminded us of God's scriptural promise to carry us through the deep waters.

After my dad died, I forced myself to get through Christmas for my family's sake. Then I fell apart. I was in such deep despair that I could not stop crying. The realization that my life would never be the same without my dad brought me to hysteria. I could not feel God's comfort. I went to see a good friend who spent the whole day with me walking in the hills, reading Scriptures, holding me, and praying with me. She listened to me and let me cry freely. I have never felt so deeply loved or accepted by a friend. She dropped everything to be God's arms around me.

An auto accident took the lives of our oldest and youngest children, leaving our middle son in ICU. Extended family, church family, even people we had never met gathered around to hold us up during the worst storm of our lives. No matter what task I faced, someone was always by my side, whether I was discussing organ donations, making funeral arrangements, staying with my son in the hospital, or talking with the media. Other friends remained at our home cleaning, cooking, and doing laundry and yard work. Certain friends took time off work to spend the night with us. People stood in the funeral receiving line for four hours just to hug us and tell us that they loved us. Another family opened their home to our remaining son for frequent visits. They know how much he misses family time with siblings and needs an escape from the grief at home.

While working in his backyard, my father died from a sudden heart attack. Nothing could have prepared me for such grief. Thoughtful gestures from my friends were so meaningful. One friend placed a flower on my porch with a note that said, *"I drove by your house today and wanted you to know I am praying for you."* A year after my dad's death, a friend gave me a handkerchief monogrammed with our family initial. Her note said, *"For all the tears you have cried this past year."* She knew how deeply I was still hurting and missing him.

When our long-awaited first baby was miscarried, my wife and I were both devastated. On Father's Day a friend stopped by and invited me to go running with him. We didn't really talk about losing the baby. He understood I needed to run off all that pain and disappointment. I needed an outlet for my grief.

Abandoned by the baby's father and feeling unable to raise a child alone, I made the heart-wrenching decision to end the pregnancy. My friend counseled me against having an abortion, but she stuck by me through the entire ordeal. She loved me unconditionally when she didn't agree with my choices. Aware that I had taken the life of my child, my guilt was overwhelming. The most helpful thing she did was listen as I poured out my grief and explained the procedure in detail. It was difficult for her to hear, but she loved me enough to walk through the pain with me.

I wanted to speak about my father at his funeral, but his unexpected death left me emotionally paralyzed and my thoughts were confused. Having lost her own father the previous year, my friend understood how I wanted to honor my dad. She listened one evening while I shared the most special things I remembered about my father. She went home and wrote the eulogy that I read at his memorial. She brought order to my inner turmoil.

As my preschooler endured the final stages of brain cancer, my friend came by every day on her way home from work, bringing food from the deli for our family. Sitting with me on the couch as I held my daughter in her fitful sleep, my friend would tell me how beautiful my daughter was. Despite the tumor that distorted my baby's face, she saw my precious child beneath the ugly cancer that was destroying her life.

My daughter had dreamed of receiving a bouquet of roses on her birthday, but she was killed in an auto accident just before she turned sixteen. My dear friend sent sixteen roses to the funeral to stand beside my daughter's casket. Her thoughtfulness meant so much to me.

My own father had recently died when we began caring for my father-in-law. He had lung cancer and wanted to die in his home. My husband and I spent most of our time at my father-in-law's home. Aware of our exhaustion and that our teenagers were grieving the loss of their grandfathers, friends sent us a gift certificate to a local dining service that would bring meals to our home from any restaurant in town plus a movie video of our choice. This was the perfect rest and refreshment for a drained family.

Being childless is an invisible but very painful loss. Some people assume that we consider our careers more important than having children. Others interrogate us with probing personal questions about our fertility. We desperately wanted children of our own but were unable to conceive. The adoption process was disappointing. As we were finally about to bring a baby home from the hospital, the birth mother changed her mind at the last minute. Emotionally we couldn't go through that again. One friend didn't ask lots of questions. Instead, she included us in her family holiday celebrations and remembered us on Mother's Day and Father's Day. In a million ways she let us know we weren't alone with our empty arms.

After our daughter's funeral, we were emotionally, physically, and spiritually drained. Friends encouraged us to take a vacation before returning to our daily routine without our daughter. They arranged for us to visit another family who had lost their son the previous year. We were able to rest, experience a change of scenery, and still be with people who understood our grief. That refreshment for our broken souls was critical.

My husband's death at age twenty-five left me a young widow with a toddler. Too devastated to envision a future without my partner, I couldn't bear to hear my toddler calling for his daddy. My first reaction was to remove all painful reminders by taking down my husband's photos in the house and giving away his belongings. My husband's uncle gently helped me see that my toddler still needed a daddy, even a deceased one. No matter how painful it was for me, my toddler needed to see his daddy's photos and hear stories about him. My husband's uncle encouraged me to save my husband's special belongings to pass on to my son when he was older. Now that my son is a young man, those possessions mean everything to him. Though it was difficult for me to keep my husband's memory alive daily, it was critical to my son's well-being. That dear uncle helped us carry our grief and preserve a heritage for my son.

In the midst of an unusually trying time, a bouquet of flowers arrived at my door. The giver explained that she honored her deceased mother every year on her mother's birthday by sending flowers to someone who exhibited the qualities she most admired in her mother. I was touched and encouraged to share that legacy.

I have AIDS and I am dying. As the son of a pastor, I doubted my family could ever understand my struggles. Fearing they would disown me if they learned my secret, I became an expert at hiding my homosexual lifestyle. Contracting AIDS forced me to tell my parents and siblings the truth. To my surprise, they wrapped me in unconditional love and are caring for me during my illness. Through them, I see the total love and forgiveness of Jesus Christ in a way I never understood before.

When others would avoid mentioning the name of

my deceased child, one friend would speak about my child frequently. She opened the door for me to share and relive our memories often. This was very comforting. On the anniversary of my child's death from leukemia, she encouraged me to enter a walk-athon with her to raise money for leukemia research. We have done this annually for years now. I appreciate being able to do something productive to honor my child's memory on that painful anniversary, and thanks to my dear friend, I don't have to do it alone.

The accidental death of my father and brother left me an angry, hurting teenager. My world fell apart overnight. It tore me up inside to see my mother cry. I dreaded coming home to a quiet, somber house at the end of every day. My best friend's family invited me over for dinner often. Having meals with his four active siblings was always an adventure. His dad was a crazy, funny man just like my dad had been, and I was able to laugh again. His mom made me feel like part of their family. Today as an adult, I realize how difficult being alone must have been for my mom, and I hope that her friends reached out to her on those lonely nights when I couldn't deal with my own pain, much less hers.

When my young wife died in a car accident, I was left with two small daughters to care for. I felt lost and devastated. I didn't know how I would go on. Who would take care of my children when I tried to return to work? Despite their own intense grief, my wife's parents immediately stepped in to daily take care of our children. I know how difficult and painful this was for all of us. It was an especially hard transition when I remarried years later. I will always be grateful to them.

Our baby was terminally ill. During those precious and terrible last weeks of my child's life, I was never alone. Friends and neighbors made sure someone was always quietly and peacefully in the house with me. Throughout the ordeal, they gave me the gift of presence.

When words are most empty, tears are most apt.
—MAX LUCADO

CHAPTER FOUR

In Times of Famine

Seasons of famine in our lives can be caused by broken relationships, financial struggles, or periods of severe stress.

If one should fall, the other helps him up; but woe to the man by himself with no one to help him up when he falls down.

—ECCLESIASTES 4:10 NJB

When my friend lived nearby, she would leave pots of homemade soup at my front door. Though she now lives across the country, distance has not changed our relationship. Whenever either of us is in the midst of a difficult time, we send "love in a box." Comfort spills out of care packages filled with cards, magazine clippings, books, teas, candy, recipes, and other gifts of cheer. We definitely feel hugged by a God who isn't limited by the distance between us.

After my divorce, I was unable to take care of the yard the way my husband had, nor could I afford to hire a gardener. My friend came every week to take care of my yard, free of charge.

Christmas was approaching, and my husband had been unemployed many months. Friends from church left a love offering on our porch, complete with money donations and numerous coupons to be used in town. God sustained us through their gift.

My relationship with extended family has always been tumultuous. The time came when they completely cut ties, and we were not even invited for Thanksgiving. I felt rejected and unwanted. My friend invited us to her home, saying that we would be their "Thanksgiving family." We had a wonderful time without any family conflicts, and the tradition continued for years. Now I look for others who do not have a place to go and welcome them into our home for holiday dinners.

When my son was struggling to learn to read, my friend began writing letters to him. Having a pen pal inspired him to write back to her. Later my friend sent my son a magazine subscription featuring his favorite hobby. Reading became a special bond between them and the prescription for his future success.

After twenty years of marriage, I was devastated when my husband suddenly left. It was difficult for me to get out of bed every morning. I later learned that the man who delivered my newspaper prayed for me each morning as he left the paper at my door.

My husband's weekly business travel had strained our relationship. Time alone together was rare. We never felt good about leaving our children for some getaway time, because they didn't see their dad all week, either. My friend sent an invitation for dinner at her home, enclosing gift certificates to the local movie theater. After a relaxing meal, my friend entertained our children at her home while my husband and I went to the show. We enjoyed a much needed retreat, knowing our children had been included in the fun.

Often a church family will provide meals during the birth of a new baby, death of a loved one, severe illness, or other major life crises. But what about the little crises? When I would be pressed for time or energy, my friend would leave me a "rescue meal" on the porch—a pot of soup or pasta and sauce, a loaf of bread, and a yummy sweet treat. I knew that she cared about my situation.

When I returned to work after going through a divorce, I came home too late and too exhausted each evening to fix the meals I once did for my children. One day my friend collaborated with my teenage daughter to have dinner waiting in the oven for me as a surprise when I came home from work. Just the aroma that greeted me as I entered the door encouraged my heart.

It had been a chaotic summer. My husband had been traveling constantly, and breaks from the duties at home were rare for me. Knowing I would decline any invitation, as I didn't have the energy to arrange for child care, my pastor told me to block out an afternoon. His wife took me out to an elegant lunch while our pastor took our children on a bike ride and picnic. I have never forgotten that loving gesture and how they practiced what they preached.

Our family was happy to bring my husband's ailing grandmother home to live with us, but her need for round-the-clock care soon left me emotionally and physically drained. A lady from church saw my need and arranged to come to my home twice a week to sit with Granny while I went to the dentist, doctor, grocery store, or out for lunch with my children. By providing these breaks, she helped our time with Granny to be pleasant rather than burdensome.

My husband and I had been preparing to divorce for months, but the day he actually moved out was wrenching. After his moving van pulled away, my friend brought over a bouquet of flowers, recognizing my pain and the new beginning in my life.

I always dreaded long car trips with our family. Returning to my parents' home for Thanksgiving was particularly difficult because it was the anniversary of my dad's death. During our visit the year before, Dad had suddenly died. A friend gave us a travel care package with snacks for the trip and activities to pass the time. She recognized what a painful trip it was, and she was going with us in her heart.

Emotionally bankrupt, I faced the fact that I had been in an abusive marriage for fifteen years. I finally told a friend how serious my situation was and started seeing a counselor. My friend cared for my preschooler during my weekly appointment and always had a delicious lunch waiting for me when I returned, exhausted and drained. Without her to hold me up, I doubt that I would have survived that arduous time.

Out of work for several months, we were driving across the country to interview for a potential job. We had very little cash, not even enough to buy fast-food meals for our three children. A woman must have overheard us talking as we stood in line at the restaurant, because she pressed money into my husband's hand and said she enjoyed helping families. Then she was gone. We felt certain an angel had fed us that day.

During my senior year in high school, I sat crying through my final exam in history class. Instead of being upset with me, my teacher called me outside the classroom to ask what was wrong. I told him that my boyfriend had been unfaithful. Coming from a home without supportive parents, I had wrapped up my life in my boyfriend and now felt like I'd been thrown away. My teacher simply asked, "What do YOU want in life?" No one had ever asked me that before. He suggested that I use this breakup as an opportunity to follow my dreams and start over. He encouraged me to attend college. Four days later, I moved across the state, enrolled in college courses, and started a new life. My life was changed because one person cared.

My marriage is less than ideal. I have been helped the most by friends who refrain from giving advice but instead offer books and similar resources, saying, "I thought you might be interested in this." These gifts equip me with positive tools to deal with my unique situation.

I was devastated when I learned that my unwed teenage daughter was pregnant. Grieving the death of her bright future, I felt like a failure as a parent.

A friend wrote me a letter listing all the ways that I had been a good mother. I needed that affirmation.

⁂

I grew up in a home where I was emotionally and physically abused by my mother and sexually abused by my father. Our parents were happy to have us out of the house on Sundays when my sisters and I attended the church across the street. The pastor and his wife welcomed me into their home regularly and adopted me as a big sister/baby-sitter to their own children. As they made me feel like a part of their family, I saw for the first time that other families were not like my own. They treated each other with love, kindness, and respect. The love of this family changed my life; they gave me a vision and a hope for a better future with Jesus Christ.

⁂

The day my husband moved out, our neighbors immediately invited my children and me to come for dinner that night. It would have been very difficult to be sitting around our own table that evening. Their hospitality helped ease the loneliness of that transition.

⁂

My husband's parents are deceased, and my parents have chosen not to be involved in our children's lives. I longed to have extended family to share in our children's special events. We have now been blessed with adoptive grandparents who make it a priority to attend our children's music recitals, church plays, birthdays, and other important events. Not having grandchildren of their own, perhaps these treasured friends need us as much as we need them. God truly places the lonely in families of His own design.

After my parents divorced, Mom and I struggled to make ends meet. Car maintenance was not a priority. I worked at a deli, and one of my customers from the service station next door offered to fill my gas tank during his break. After filling the tank, he gave our car a complete service and tune-up and refused to accept a dime for his services. He became a dear family friend.

I had an addiction problem and my wife and children finally left me. That same night a group of men from our church came to lovingly confront me regarding the behavior that had destroyed my family. These men prayed with me, recommended

counseling, and pledged to walk with me every step
as I repented and worked to rebuild all that I had
destroyed. They stayed in daily contact with me
through the recovery process. Today I am grateful
to be in recovery and reconciled with my family.

As a long-distance truck driver, I am away from
home on a regular basis. My wife has two friends
who stay in constant contact with her when I am
on the road. Our church provides me with tapes of
the recorded services that I can listen to while I am
driving. This makes me feel like I am still a part of
the church family.

I did not have any support systems when my husband went to prison. The church my children had
occasionally attended reached out to us. Every
Sunday the church van picked up my children for
Sunday school and invited me to come along. The
pastor visited my husband in prison and regularly
wrote letters to him. Our new church family provided financial help, car maintenance, clothes, and
special outings for my children. It wasn't long before I dedicated my life to the Lord and joined a
Christian support group for wives of inmates. I no
longer felt abandoned and ashamed. Instead, I knew

I was loved and God was taking care of us.

Financial struggles were a way of life for us. My friend was in the same situation, and we traded coupons, outgrown clothing, furniture—anything that would help ease the burden of the other. It was a precious friendship born out of crisis. When my friend was able to buy groceries through a network for low-income families, she brought me a bag of groceries, including chocolate chips! Baking chocolate chip cookies for my sons was one way I held on to a normal life, believing that we would be all right. The next week, my friend brought me two bags of chocolate chips. Her gifts taught me that God does care about the little things in our lives.

Having moved to another state, I was feeling lonely and homesick because we couldn't return home for the holidays. As a little girl, my favorite gift was the new doll my mother would give me each Christmas. That tradition had obviously changed now that I was an adult. But on this first Christmas away from family, my tears were transformed into a smile as I opened the gift my mom mailed to me. Inside the package I found three silly little dolls grinning up at me. Across the miles my mom knew I needed an extra dose of mothering that year.

Though I thought I was prepared, actually receiving my divorce papers was a painful experience. The loss was so final. On the day the papers arrived, I called a friend who immediately came over to cry with me. I didn't feel as alone and abandoned with my friend by my side.

I struggle with chemical depression. Anyone who suffers with depression knows that once you fall into that dark pit of hopelessness, despair, and fatigue, it is impossible to reach out for help. I have a friend who regularly calls me. She can hear in my voice if I am struggling. She never fails to find some way, whether through a gift, note, or invitation out, to pull me back to reality. My friend struggles with depression too, so she understands what I am going through and knows just how to help.

The crisis of my life has not been one specific event but the long, difficult journey of my troubled marriage. My sister-in-law is my encourager. Married to my husband's brother, she understands my struggles. There have been times when I have sobbed on the phone with her, and she never fails to listen and pray with me.

My parents divorced when I was a teenager. The first time I had to celebrate my birthday at two different homes was not a happy occasion. My best friend gave me a scrapbook with pictures of the two of us through the years. Friends since we were toddlers, we shared many beautiful memories. Her gift assured me that though some things in life change, our friendship never would. I needed that anchor.

The most difficult thing I ever had to do was find a full-time job and leave my children during the day. When my husband abandoned us, I didn't want to put my children in a day-care facility with strangers. In addition to disrupting their lives, day care was too expensive for my budget. One friend daily welcomed my children into her home to be part of their family and even provided transportation to their activities. Sometimes my friend sent a dinner home with us at the end of a long day. I paid her what I could, but I will never be able to repay her kindness. We would not have survived without her support.

My husband was right in the middle of a controversial church conflict. The most productive thing I could do was keep quiet, stay out of the mess, and not add to the problem. Because some people had stopped speaking to my husband, and to me as well, I began to feel misunderstood, alone, and invisible. Then one friend from church showed up on my doorstep and said, "I want to know how YOU are." Her question made me feel loved and cared about through a difficult ordeal.

Because I am a single mom with three children, I cannot go out at night like my friends who have husbands at home watching their children. I must say no to many church and social gatherings. Most people learn that I am unavailable and just stop thinking of me. But one friend sometimes brings me dinner or a special dessert from a restaurant after she has been out with our mutual friends. I appreciate that she remembers my situation and brings the party to me.

Due to an addiction problem, my husband was in and out of work. I felt like a failure trying to keep our family together. My daughter's school tuition was due and I didn't have it. When I went to the school to remove my daughter from the program, her teacher told me the tuition had been paid by an anonymous friend. Another friend sent me checks for small amounts throughout the year, each arriving the week I needed to buy something. God constantly delivered the message that I was not alone.

When my son went to prison, I was brokenhearted. The despair was indescribable. With very few exceptions, no one knew what to say or how to ease my grief. Many were quick to judge. One friend left a candy bar or other sweet treat on my desk at work once a week for the length of my son's prison term. Another friend left flowers. They didn't have to say anything. I knew they cared about me. I knew they prayed for my son.

I felt betrayed and humiliated when I learned that my husband was having an affair with my friend. I needed a safe place where I could talk and cry, but it didn't help when others would say bad things about my husband. I was most encouraged when supportive friends would say, "We love you both, and we are praying for both of you. We know this is hard."

When I was experiencing years of repeated loss along with the pain caused by rebellious teens, I had a friend who was my safe place. She was literally the arms of Christ around me. Even when I was angry and verbally brutal, she listened without judging. She didn't pretend to have any answers. She gently encouraged me to follow God through the pain, and she helped me laugh again. When I needed to hibernate, she would let me disappear for a while. My friend made no demands on me. She was there when I needed her, and she loved me unconditionally.

My husband is an active man, immersed in his work and hobbies and leading activities at church. He never stops moving, which puts a strain on our relationship. He is unable to videotape activities he is directing, and I am not very mechanical. Without passing judgment on our situation, one friend regularly videotapes our children's performances and gives the tapes and photographs to us as gifts throughout the year. We call her our "family historian." My children will have a legacy of memories because of this special friend's faithful involvement in our lives.

The last few months of my doctoral program were extremely stressful. I had to give a solo recital in addition to surviving doctoral exams, orals, and a dissertation defense. Being a shy person made the entire process paralyzing for me. A group of my friends organized a rotating prayer watch. Each woman diligently prayed for me for fifteen minutes of each presentation I gave. Thanks to their support, I survived the pressure cooker. That degree belongs to all of us.

When my husband was discharged from military service, we found ourselves jobless and homeless. I took our four small children to stay at a friend's mountain cabin while my husband looked for employment in another state. Isolated and on the edge of despair, life looked hopeless. I even thought about suicide. Though we weren't his responsibility anymore, our former military base chaplain tracked me down. He spent time with me on the phone, asking serious questions to keep me focused on continuing to live. He said he would be there for me during the tough days, and he was. I'm thankful he cared enough to help me across the miles.

It never seems to fail that when my husband is traveling for business, creatures enter our house. We had a mouse invasion during one of his trips, and I was terrified of them. To scare the mice away, our pastor left a big plastic snake on my porch. That snake did console me, but most importantly, it made me laugh.

Every job has its challenging seasons. I am a teacher, so the first week of school, the last week, and report card conferences are the most stressful times of the year. One friend consistently recognizes those weeks with a meal for our family or gift certificates with notes of encouragement. I feel supported when I most need it.

Neither my husband nor I have siblings, and our parents are aging. Our children had never experienced those joyful extended family times with aunts, uncles, and cousins until my friend proclaimed herself to be my children's adopted aunt. She gives them gifts at Christmas, remembers their birthdays, and phones them on the first day of school to see how their day went. "Family" that chooses to love you is a beautiful gift.

74

I was living in a lonely, disintegrating marriage when I met a man who made me feel special again. He, too, was in a miserable marriage. As a Christian, I knew I was headed for trouble and it wouldn't be long before we were involved in an affair. An acquaintance confided that she had been involved in an extramarital affair early in her marriage. After much hard work and counseling, she and her husband remained married. She bluntly told me that the chaos and pain caused by an affair were never worth the momentary pleasure. She warned that my life would be in ruins and the harm done to my children would haunt me forever. If anyone else had said these things to me, I would have been angry with that person for preaching. But she personally understood my loneliness and loved me enough to try to protect me from the destruction she had experienced. I walked away from that potential affair. Today I may not have "happiness," but I do have God's peace. My friend risked being vulnerable and saved my life.

An alcoholic, my husband would leave the children and me for days at a time. Because I couldn't count on him, I began cleaning houses to provide for the

children. One of the families I cleaned house for
was a Christian family. Everything in their home
spoke of their faith. I could feel God's peace and
love when I walked in the door. I wanted that faith
in my life. I became a Christian, and later my husband committed his life to Christ. Today we are
raising our children in a loving Christian home,
much like the one I cleaned all those years ago.

When our business went bankrupt, we were overwhelmed with debts. My husband worked two jobs
as we struggled to pay our bills and feed our new
baby. Each week a friend brought me a coffee can
filled with pinto beans and a loaf of homemade
bread. Like the loaves and fishes, the Lord multi-
plied her simple offering and taught me a multitude
of creative recipes utilizing beans. God nourished
our family through my friend's precious generosity.

I grew up one of many children in a small home
where our alcoholic parents were constantly fight-
ing. Without enough food, money, time, or space to
go around, we children always looked for ways to
be out of the house. My best friend across the street
was an only child. Her parents made me feel that I
was part of their family. They invited me over each

week to play, have dinner, and spend the night, and they even brought me along on family vacations. They were my oasis, a retreat from my chaotic homelife.

***

Fire destroyed our home and all of our belongings. Everything could be replaced except our family photographs. One friend networked with relatives and friends to have them copy any pictures they had of our family. The photo albums she created gave us back our family history and priceless memories.

***

Suddenly unemployed, my wife and I were penniless. We could not even afford to buy a daily newspaper to study the want ads. Each morning our neighbor gave me a smile, a cup of coffee, and the classified section from the paper. I quickly found a job through those ads.

***

When I am struggling, there is always one person I can call to pray for me. I know my friend will go to her knees and earnestly ask God to strengthen and guide me. This is not a friend I see often; our social lives and daily paths rarely cross. But my personal prayer warrior's concern for me goes beyond social circles and is a critical part of my life.

While my husband was in prison, I vacillated between wanting to unconditionally love and support him, and feeling angry about the crime he committed. Every week my friend went with me to visit my husband in prison. I would not have made it through that terrible time without her support.

Through my own poor behavior choices, I lost my job, my house, and my wife. Going through that loss brought me to the brink of suicide. My mother faithfully drove out to spend time with me every weekend for four months. She had little money, but she always treated me to a meal, a movie, or a shopping trip. She sacrificed her own needs for mine. If it wasn't for my mom, I wouldn't be here today. She was a lifeline when I was drowning in despair.

Having a spouse who travels for business leaves me a single parent every week. I am constantly discouraged and exhausted. The toughest challenge comes when the alarm goes off at 3:00 A.M. on Monday morning so my husband can catch the early flight east. If I can't go back to sleep, the entire day is miserable. By nightfall I'm so tired I can barely stand, let alone face the million things I have yet to do to get the children in bed and prepare for the next day. I have one friend who will sometimes come and watch my children on Monday afternoons, enabling me to take a nap—and I feel revitalized.

Feeling quite victimized, I poured out my heart to a close friend, listing all the wrongs that my husband had inflicted on me. She gently said, "I think that you have a problem with unconditional love." She loved me enough to confront me. Her words changed my perspective. As I accepted my husband, my marriage began to heal.

After months of unemployment, finances were tight and we were discouraged. During Christmas week, my friend gave me a festive tablecloth. Tucked inside the tablecloth were gift certificates to our local market. The tablecloth would have been useless without something to put on it. My friend provided a feast of the heart that fed us physically and emotionally.

My grown son was angry and troubled. His behavior caused constant turmoil in our family. When the situation would once again overwhelm me, I would phone my friends or go to their home. That couple's prayers, affirmations, and belief in my son's potential and in my vision for his future equipped me to keep my eyes on the goal.

Our neighborhood was evacuated as wildfire ravaged acres of land around our home. God protected our house, but our entire yard was destroyed. A family who lived hours away loaded up their Rototiller, plant starts from their own yard, and handfuls of seeds. They spent the day landscaping our yard. Those friends literally turned our ashes to beauty when we were too drained to face the future.

Suppose a brother or sister is without clothes and daily food. If one of you says to him, "Go, I wish you well; keep warm and well fed," but does nothing about his physical needs, what good is it?

—JAMES 2:15–16 NIV

CHAPTER FIVE

New Beginnings

A wide variety of reasons can cause us to enter unknown territory, start over again, or begin a new chapter in our life. When these times are acknowledged by others, we receive the grace and courage we need to face the future.

A generous man will prosper, he who refreshes others will himself be refreshed.

—PROVERBS 11:25 NIV

When I moved to another part of the state, I had to leave my best friend. Close as sisters, we could talk about anything and everything. I grieved the loss of our daily relationship. On our last visit together, she presented me with a beautifully wrapped package. Inside were two teacups, plates, and a matching teapot. Her note unselfishly said that though she and I would continue our friendship despite the miles between us, she knew I would need a close friend in my new city. She encouraged me to make new friends and share long talks with them too. Twenty years later, she remains one of my closest friends, and I still use those teacups when I reach out to someone new.

I was becoming a grandmother under difficult circumstances. My teenage son had fathered a child out of wedlock. Instead of a traditional grandmother shower, my friend gave me a "modern-day foot washing." She called my closest friends together to bring gifts and words of encouragement about the challenge ahead. Over afternoon tea, my friends soothed my wounds. I left knowing that I was not alone in what the future held.

I was getting married and desperately wanted my mother-in-law to accept me. At my bridal shower she presented me with a beautiful package containing a pair of apron strings. I felt wrapped in her love, acceptance, and confidence in me.

My daughter married two years after my husband died. At her request, I took her dad's place and walked my daughter down the aisle. After the honey-mooners left and the last of the rice and wedding cake was cleaned up, I reluctantly drove home to my quiet, empty house where I had lived alone since my husband's death. All the wedding plans had brought activity and houseguests back into my home as extended family and friends helped prepare for the grand event. Now I dreaded returning to my loneliness. I was surprised to find a gift basket sitting on my porch. The attached card read, *"For the Mother of the Bride."* Inside I found bubble bath, teas, chocolates, scented candles, and the video *Father of the Bride.* My friend remembered how alone and tired I would be that night. Her gift transformed my lonely evening into a cozy celebration.

The early months of my pregnancy coincided with an important business party I needed to attend with my husband. I was too ill to get out of bed, let alone shop for an appropriate outfit. One friend shopped for me, and another came to my home and styled my hair. Another friend loaned me accessories from her wardrobe. Because of their special efforts, I was able to accompany my husband and not feel embarrassed about my appearance.

I was away at college for the first time and quite homesick. I hadn't made any close friends when my birthday arrived. My family sent a birthday package complete with everything needed for a party. I invited other students in the dorm to help me celebrate, and that was the beginning of many new friendships. I discovered everyone was as homesick as I was. Across the miles, my family was still celebrating my special day.

Having just moved to a new town, I was feeling lonely and out of place. A woman I had met at our new church sent a lovely lunch invitation, complete with a gift certificate to a local restaurant. Her loving gesture was the turning point for me, and she remains one of my closest friends.

Recovering from a Caesarean section and caring for our new baby found me seriously sleep deprived. One morning we found a basket of muffins, pastries, juice, fruit, and colorful plates and napkins on our front porch. A festive balloon was tied to the basket. After a good breakfast and a hug from my friend, the day looked much brighter.

As a teenager, I gave up my illegitimate baby for adoption, a secret I kept for decades. I found my son forty-two years later. I finally got up the courage to tell a new friend about our reunion. Because her husband had been adopted, she understood and cried tears of joy with me. The next week she organized our seniors' group to give me a surprise baby shower complete with blue streamers, balloons, and a cake that read, *"It's a boy!"* Another friend videotaped the party so that I could send it to my son. I had always been painfully ashamed of my secret. The acceptance and love of my friends was healing.

After graduating early from high school, I was eager to pursue emergency medical training. Unable to afford the tuition, I decided to apply to the program and continue earning the money to enroll. One day a check from good friends arrived in the mail—a scholarship for the entire course. Because they believed in me enough to fund my dream, they have inspired me to do the best I can.

When I was promoted at work, my wife contacted others who had experience in my new position. She asked each of them to write me a letter containing their advice pertaining both to the job and to my spiritual walk. That wise counsel from those who had gone before me was priceless.

We moved across the country a few weeks before our sixth child was born. We were missing our previous church and their practice of celebrating the arrival of each child in the congregation with a baby shower. I wanted this child to be welcomed by our church family as joyously as our other children had been. Shortly after the birth of our baby, a large package arrived by mail. The women from our previous church had sent a "baby shower in a box." Gifts were tucked around a videotape. I cried as I watched the video, seeing my friends holding up their gifts to the camera and welcoming our new child.

I was a divorcee and engaged to be married to a man who was also divorced. We knew that remarriage for divorced people was a controversial issue in some churches. We began attending the church where we planned to be married. Some of our new friends there organized a wedding shower for us, just like they would for a first marriage. They made us feel accepted and loved.

It was a bittersweet transition when my children left for college. I was so proud of my children's achievements, yet I grieved losing them in my daily life. Leaving my firstborn at school was traumatic, yet leaving my "baby" was even more difficult because I returned to an empty nest. My main job was essentially finished. A friend who had a key to my house left a special gift in my entryway. Attached to a packet of seeds was a note that read, *"This is what you started with."* Beside that was a lovely flowering plant with another note, *"Congratulations on your daughter's blossoming."* She turned a dreaded moment into a beautiful homecoming.

Our new neighbors welcomed us to the neighborhood with a cheery basket filled with fixings for a "moving dinner," accompanied by an invitation to come over for coffee once we were settled. One family reached out to make us feel like we belonged.

Our twins were born prematurely and remained in the neonatal ICU for two months. I was constantly torn between being at the hospital with the struggling twins and being home with my other children who needed me. Two friends together prepared thirty meals to put in our freezer, complete with cooking instructions easy enough for my children to follow. No matter how chaotic the day had been, we had a delicious hot dinner every night. Our friends nourished our bodies as well as our souls.

I felt very homesick when I moved to a new town and my birthday passed unacknowledged by new acquaintances. Six months later a special friend gave me a big half-birthday party. That celebration made me feel loved and was the turning point in my adjustment to a new life.

I discovered I was pregnant in April. Being unmarried, I felt scared and alone. I knew how disappointed my family was in me. On Mother's Day, a friend brought me a baby shower in a basket to celebrate my first Mother's Day. In addition to gifts for the baby, she included one coupon to be my coach during labor and delivery, another coupon for future baby-sitting, and another for a delivered meal. Though the circumstances were less than ideal, I realized that new life is always something to celebrate. I was not facing my pregnancy alone; this baby would be loved.

When a fellow member of our pastoral staff prepared to transfer to another congregation, our church surrounded his family with the traditional send-off parties, gifts, and well-wishes. While the focus of excitement and attention centered on the pastor who was leaving, I was trying to adjust to the changing dynamics his absence would mean to the rest of us on staff and to the church. At one farewell function, a young couple hugged me and slipped an envelope into my hand. Inside was a note for my wife and me expressing their appreciation for our continuing ministry to them in our present location and a gift certificate to our favorite restaurant.

For my eighteenth birthday, my parents celebrated my coming of age with a surprise party. They invited everyone who had positively influenced me as I was growing up. Each guest took a moment to write down their best piece of advice and favorite Scripture. Those keepsake notes have continued to guide and inspire me.

We had moved across the country and felt lost in our new neighborhood. One neighbor took us on a driving tour of the area, pointing out the library, various stores, churches, doctors' offices, and more. That hour saved me much time later when I would have been driving around lost. Another neighbor invited us over for the afternoon. She included all the women who lived on our block. My children had a great time playing with their children. That afternoon established a support network that I still rely on. Those neighbors didn't give me time to wallow in my loneliness.

After graduating from college, I made the difficult decision to take a job on the other side of the country. Concerned about leaving family and friends, I began to wonder if I had made the right decision. One friend left a bottle of champagne for me with a note that read, *"Ships are safe in the harbor, but that's not what ships are for."* She was "christening" me on my maiden voyage. It was just the encouragement I needed to take that step and begin a wonderful new chapter in my life.

Our world was rocked when our teenage daughter became pregnant from a single sexual experience.

Working full-time, I was no more prepared to become a grandmother than she was ready to become a mother. My friends took turns bringing lunch to my daughter at home while I was away at work. It gave me great peace of mind to know that my daughter was eating well and being checked on by people who cared about us during a difficult ordeal.

Through the years, I have tried to welcome new neighbors moving into our neighborhood by leaving a care package on their front porch with our name and phone number attached so they can contact us if they ever need help. Sometimes I receive a phone call, other times I never hear from them. One new neighbor surprised me by baking a cake for us. She baked cakes for all the neighbors around her to introduce herself, and over the years she has brought us delicious pies and other desserts for no special reason. I call her the "neighborhood angel." She has lifted my spirits many times and inspired me with her generosity of spirit and ability to reach out to others. She taught me that being the new kid on the block doesn't mean waiting for others to approach first. The opportunity works both ways.

For the past several years on the morning of my birthday, I have opened my front door to find a motorcycle parked in the driveway with the key in the ignition. A young man who had previously been a part of the youth group I lead lends me his motorcycle each year for a week. He knows I enjoy motorcycles but that it would be an impractical thing for me to own. His unique gift has spoken volumes to me, letting me know he appreciates my ministry, that he recognizes my particular interests, and that he trusts me as his friend.

Help one another to carry these heavy loads, and in this way you will fulfill the law of Christ.
—GALATIANS 6:2 NEB

CHAPTER SIX

"Don't Unhelp Me"

Be not far from me, for trouble is near,
and I have no helper.

—PSALM 22:11 NEB

When I was a child, I remember my mom busily preparing for a dinner party, saying, "If you are not going to help me, then at least don't unhelp me." This principle certainly applies to helping people in crisis. Sometimes we can do more damage than good.

To comfort is defined as "to strengthen, bring relief, encourage, or ease one's grief and suffering." Do we truly comfort those in pain? Do they feel Jesus' arms around them through our caring? Do we help spare them sorrow upon sorrow? Do they feel built up or pulled down?

In the book of Job, God takes a very hard line with "unhelpers." Job endured unimaginable pain and loss. He was stripped of his home, his health, and the support of his friends and spouse, and he lost his ten children when severe wind crushed the house around them. Brokenhearted, Job poured out his grief and despair, yet he never stopped trusting God. Job begged his friends, "Listen to me, do but listen, and let that be the comfort you offer me" (Job 21:2 NEB). But Job's friends called his pleadings the "long-winded ramblings of an old man" (Job 8:2 NEB) and even blamed Job for his tragedy: "My heart failed me when you said, 'What a train of disaster he has brought on himself! The root of the trouble lies in him' " (Job 19:27–28 NEB).

The book of Job is our best example of "unhelping." Job's friends did not help carry Job's burden; they only increased it. And God "burned with anger" against Job's friends (Job 42:7). Some of our contributors have shared what did not help them:

When my wife died, an acquaintance said, "God must have needed another angel in heaven, another flower in his garden." It is not comforting to have God reduced to a selfish, needy deity who must take from us. He is God.

After my children were killed in an auto accident, people would see me around town, glance at me, then turn away. I knew they felt awkward and didn't know what to say, but avoiding me caused more pain. All they had to say was, "Hello, I've been thinking about you. I don't know what to say," and give me a hug.

Following my miscarriage, people would say, "At least you have other children" or "God probably took the baby because there was something wrong with it" or "At least you didn't get to know this child" or "At least you are healthy and will probably conceive again." After my grandfather died, my grandmother told me that friends said, "At least you had all those years together." Don't say AT LEAST. Don't try to minimize someone's pain. It only insults the griever.

Recovering from surgery, I learned that sometimes people felt they didn't know me well enough to help. Others thought that since they didn't help immediately, they had missed their opportunity and felt awkward about contacting me. Never think it is too late to offer support, and don't assume that everyone else is helping.

When my son was murdered, acquaintances and even strangers asked us personal, probing questions about the circumstances surrounding his death. This was hurtful and intrusive. It was almost as if they wanted to find something wrong with us to assure themselves that this tragedy wouldn't happen to their family.

In my eighty years I have lost my husband, my parents, my siblings, and one child. My advice to helpers would be, "Don't make me talk when I don't feel like talking, and don't be afraid to be with me when I do." Two big mistakes that people make are: (1) asking too many questions when the griever doesn't have the energy to answer, and (2) running scared when the griever finally breaks down and needs to scream or cry.

My son, who had Down's syndrome, died when he was twenty years old. A relative said, "What a blessing. He is better off now." I wondered if her twenty-two-year-old son would be "better off" if he were dead and if that would bless her. Does an IQ make one life worth living more than another? Does an IQ change a mother's grief? I had cared for my precious, loving son his entire life, and I desperately

missed him and his daily hugs. Many thought I
would be relieved. Very few people understood my
loss, and I felt very alone in my grieving.

⁂

When I lost my wife, friends and family imposed
what they thought was "best" for me. They tried to
keep me busy and distracted when I wanted to be
alone to grieve. They made decisions for me based
on their own experiences and personalities. I wish
someone had asked me what I wanted and respected
my views. No one can grieve for you. You can't walk
around grief. You have to walk straight through it.

⁂

I have experienced intense grief in raising difficult
teenagers. It is discouraging to be given quick advice
or asked questions about our situation. I will talk to
people who I know genuinely care about me when I
am ready. Quotes such as "God won't give you
more than you can handle" or "All things work to
gether for good" sound callous and flippant.

⁂

Our young daughter, who was dying from leukemia, loved to read. When we took her to the oph-
thalmologist for a new pair of glasses, he said, "She's
going to die soon anyway. Don't waste your money

on a new prescription." He didn't understand that dying children need to make every day count and live to the fullest the life they have left.

When my best friend died, I certainly understood that her husband and children needed the most support. I was the person everyone contacted to find out what kind of help the family needed. Yet no one seemed to understand how deeply I was grieving. I needed comfort, too. My advice is to look beyond the immediate family when someone dies and be aware of other outside grievers.

People were quick with medical and fertility advice after our second miscarriage. My husband and I needed time to process our grief. We had neither the emotional nor physical strength to consider our options right away. I needed friends to give me a hug and say, "I'm sorry. I've been there and I know how you feel." Later I would be ready for them to say, "By the way, this might be of interest to you."

My first day back to work after my mother's funeral, a co-worker said, "I know just how you feel. My cat died recently." How could someone compare my mother's major role in my life with a cat? It would have been more sensitive to simply say, "I'm sorry."

───※───

Anxious to fix me and help me get over my loss quickly, well-meaning friends came to sort out and pack away my husband's clothes after his death. They didn't understand that I needed to do that as part of my grief work, remembering everything about him. In trying to spare me pain, they robbed me of ways I could work through my grief and only delayed the process.

───※───

Sometimes loss brings a couple closer, but in the case of losing a child, it usually drives spouses apart. Two drowning people cannot save each other. The divorce rate is high for parents who have lost a child. Our marriage deteriorated after our daughter died. We didn't have the time or money to seek help. No one seemed to see how serious our situation was and divorce was inevitable. I wish now that someone had helped us seek counseling.

PLEASE

PLEASE, don't ask me if I'm over it yet. I'll never be over it.

PLEASE, don't tell me she's in a better place.
She isn't here with me.
PLEASE, don't say at least she isn't suffering.
I haven't come to terms with why she had to suffer at
*   all.*
PLEASE, don't tell me you know how I feel
Unless you have lost a child.
PLEASE, don't ask me if I feel better.
Bereavement isn't a condition that clears up.
PLEASE, don't tell me at least you had her for so many
*   years.*
What year would you choose for your child to die?
PLEASE, don't tell me God never gives us more than we
*   can bear.*
PLEASE, just say you are sorry.
PLEASE, just say you remember my child, if you do.
PLEASE, just let me talk about my child.
PLEASE, mention my child's name.
PLEASE, just let me cry.

—Rita Moran
  Compassionate Friends

CHAPTER SEVEN

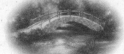

Coming Alongside—A Paraclete Ministry

Reading these chapters, you probably noticed that the most meaningful help rarely came in the form of an organized program but usually came in the context of a relationship. Church activities, theological knowledge, and a host of traditional church programs cannot guarantee spontaneous, caring community and intimate, mutual relationships. It is nearly impossible to notice someone's pain without being in a relationship with that person. Helping begins with seeing and being aware of the changes in someone's life.

God connects people in powerful, miraculous ways. PeggySue and I have observed care groups and Bible study groups, inspired by the Holy Spirit, that connect members in intimate relationships where authentic community and true helping occurred. Other programs seem to miss the mark. They are artificial, seeming only to go through the motions. These programs meet social needs but fail to provide a safe place for sharing intimate struggles. Actions apart from a caring relationship are empty and devoid of meaning. They are functional. Receiving a phone call or a meal as a result of being assigned to someone's list does not always make the recipient feel hugged by God. Our contributors showed us that what is done is not nearly as important as how it is done.

If structured groups are sometimes unnatural ways for people to relate, then how can the church help hurting people who do not have support systems and fall through the cracks? Church programs are only as effective as they are instrumental in encouraging relationships. These are the thoughts that rattled around in my brain when I was given the opportunity, with the support of our deaconess board, to develop a program to encourage natural, ministering relationships. We called it the Paraclete Ministry, giving church members the opportunity to come alongside and support one another. We simply wanted to open the door and get out of God's way.

Our philosophy was based on three principles: (1) the church is a hospital for people who hurt, a home for the broken; (2) people are naturally bonded together by shared pain; and (3) caring begins with understanding.

First we studied the relevant issues and struggles in our congregation. Where did our people hurt? We held monthly panel discussions for one year with each meeting based on a specific topic, including:

- Living with serious illness
- Parenting challenging children
- Living with our emotions: anger, depression, and fear
- Survivors of abusive and dysfunctional backgrounds
- Grief and loss
- Challenging marriages
- Living the single lifestyle in a married world
- Managing stress: balancing career, family, and church demands

On each panel, six to eight people shared their experiences on the selected topic. Different perspectives were valued. We encouraged people from our church as well as the community to attend. These meetings were not intended to be therapy sessions or support groups. Anyone struggling with the same issue or interested in learning more about it to support others was welcome.

A man living with diabetes, a parent raising a developmentally disabled child, a recent widow, a single parent, a woman who had been sexually abused as a child, another who had an alcoholic father, a man going through a divorce, a woman in a difficult marriage, someone with a terminal disease—these were just a few of those who were able to share their stories. One woman, dying of cancer, was too ill to attend the meeting, so she sent a tape. This tape was treasured by her family after her death.

Our most important rule was that the meetings would be safe places to share. We would respect each other's pain and privacy. No information would be carried from the meeting. It was confidential.

Books, reading lists, and organization information for each topic was offered on a resource table. Anyone interested in participating in a regular support network or group based on the discussed issue was encouraged to sign up. Due to busy schedules, people were rarely interested in a regular meeting commitment, but they did connect one-on-one with another participant. A facilitator closed each meeting with questions, short discussion, and prayer. Refreshments followed to allow participants time to spend with one another.

The most significant outcome of the program was the new understanding participants had for one another. A common response was, "I have known that person for years and now finally understand what he struggles with and why he responds the way he does." Understanding is the key to developing relationships, the door to genuine caring.

Ideally each of us would have natural support relationships to carry us through the crises of our lives, but the church can be instrumental in offering a "coming alongside" ministry to encourage those relationships.

With deepest thanks to the following deaconesses for coming alongside to help implement the Paraclete Ministry: Debbie Fretwell, Isabel Harrison, Patty Johnsen, Ramona Palmer, Debbie Sawyer, Kris Simonsen, and Cyndi Wolke.

A Final Word

PeggySue and I want to leave you travelers on the road of helping with one final note of enCOURAGEment. No one can help everyone. I am often overwhelmed with the crises I see in the lives of people around me. Everywhere I turn, I observe a way that I could be reaching out to help someone. At times I have several friends simultaneously going through very serious crises. I want to be there for each one, but there aren't enough hours in the day. We can't meet everyone's needs, much less their desires. And we all prefer to be givers of help rather than the recipients. We don't want to add our own burdens to the burdens of our friends. It can be a double bind. Mutual, caring relationships are ideal but not that common.

A stressful schedule with numerous demands, our own family crises, a husband who travels weekly in his business, three active children, and my work leave me feeling that there is not enough of me to go around. I feel like a failure at every turn. I can barely manage my own life, much less help carry someone else's load. Caring for our own families is our first priority. Sacrificing the needs of our own children and spouses does not help anyone and simply leaves more wreckage. It is a delicate balancing act.

Yet true helping, being that miraculous link of compassion, is the work of God himself through His Holy Spirit. Even in the midst of our own struggles and busy lives we can be God's messengers of hope. Prayerfully seeking His guidance, God shows us a clear and natural path to help a few specific people He wants us to comfort. It will not be a mystery or an overwhelming task. One act of kindness inspired by these pages can be the loving arms of Jesus to a broken spirit. This circle of ministry will be ever changing. God promises to go before us to lead us and follow behind to protect and uphold us. "But you will not leave in haste or go in flight; for the Lord will go before you, the God of Israel will be your rear guard" (Isaiah 52:12 NIV). We are gratefully amazed at how God touches lives and loves people through our frail human hands.

> *God comforts us not to make us comfortable*
> *but to make us comforters.*
> —JOHN HENRY JOWETT

CONSOLATION FOR TIMES OF MOURNING

Compassionate and ultimately hopeful, these two
books offer tender words and caring wisdom for
those in grief. Like the strong hug of a loved one or
the kind words of a friend, the books present the
words you need to hear in the most thoughtful of
ways.

Grieving: Our Path Back to Peace
by James R. White

People in grief wonder if they will ever feel okay again.
For all people who experience loss, moments of joy and
normalcy mix with sadness and anger. But being
moved again by painful feelings you thought you'd
tamed isn't a setback. Rather it is part of an upward
process of healing, combined with hope in God is
ultimately your path back to peace.

When Someone You Love Is Dying
by David Clark, Ph.D.
and Peter Emmett M.D.

In a world of high-tech medicine, the approaching
death of a loved one thrusts complex decisions on
many families. For those struggling with an end-of-life
decision, this book offers biblically sound advice and
step-by-step answers regarding emergency and ongoing
medical options.

BETHANY HOUSE PUBLISHERS
11400 Hampshire Ave. South
Minneapolis, MN 55438

www.bethanyhouse.com

Available from your nearest Christian bookstore (800) 991-7747 or from Bethany House Publishers

Thank you for selecting a book from
BETHANY HOUSE PUBLISHERS

Bethany House Publishers is a ministry of Bethany Fellowship
International, an interdenominational, nonprofit organization
committed to spreading the Good News of Jesus Christ around
the world through evangelism, church planting, literature
distribution, and care for those in need. Missionary training is
offered through Bethany College of Missions.

Bethany Fellowship International is a member of the National
Association of Evangelicals and subscribes to its statement of
faith. If you would like further information, please contact:

Bethany Fellowship International
6820 Auto Club Road
Minneapolis, MN 55438 USA